Stephanie 2009

Contents:

For my mother
who taught me by her lamp

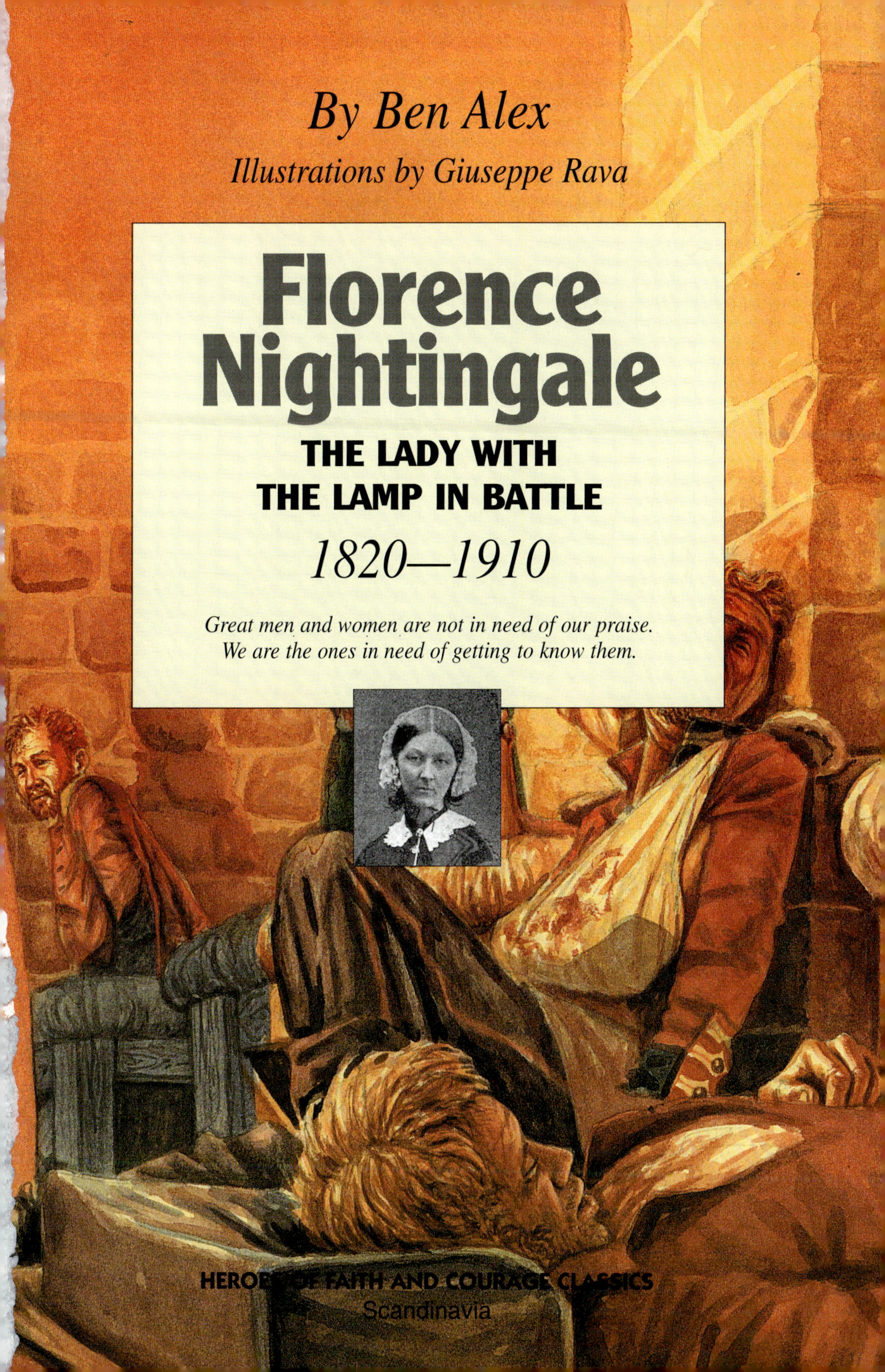

By Ben Alex

Illustrations by Giuseppe Rava

Florence Nightingale

THE LADY WITH THE LAMP IN BATTLE

1820—1910

Great men and women are not in need of our praise.
We are the ones in need of getting to know them.

HEROES OF FAITH AND COURAGE CLASSICS
Scandinavia

A DISCONTENTED DAUGHTER

"Flo! Are you daydreaming again? Hurry up! It's time to dress for dinner! The guests will arrive in less than an hour!"

Florence turned from the window and caught a glimpse of her sister Parthe already disappearing down the hall. A tired smile passed over her pale face.

"Yes, I'm coming," she sighed and tucked her book under the pillow. As soon as she was dressed she hurried downstairs to help her mother and Parthe with the last-minute preparations before the guests began to pour in.

Florence had many aunts, uncles, cousins and friends who seemed to enjoy every opportunity for a family party. In a few days the Nightingale family would leave Lea Hurst, their summer country home in Derbyshire,

and move to their other country home, Embley Park, in Hampshire. And as was the custom in their wealthy family, relatives and friends had been invited to the good-bye party.

Florence's sister Parthe enjoyed these parties more than Florence. Parthe took after her mother, throwing herself wholeheartedly into the games and dances. Florence was of a quieter nature, although she, too, enjoyed good company and interesting conversation.

That night Florence's father, William Nightingale, watched his younger daughter from behind the smoke of his long Danish pipe. He could see her dancing, and she seemed to be enjoying herself. But William knew that his favorite daughter was deeply troubled to a point where her health actually suffered. Something was bothering her. And William did not know what to do about it.

A CALL IN THE NIGHT

After the party, as the mansion at Lea Hurst grew dark and quiet, candlelight shone through the window of Florence's bedroom on the second floor. The troubled young woman sat at the table by the window with her dearest companion, her journal. She dipped the pen into the ink and wrote, "O weary days! O evenings that seem never to end! For how many long years have I watched that drawing-room clock and thought it would never reach ten!"

She flicked through the book and read some past entries.

"July 16, 1835: Spent the day arranging flowers.

". . . September 17, 1836: Took a carriage ride with Mother.

". . . October 14, 1836: Tried to paint a scene with watercolors. Horrible results!

". . . January 10, 1837: Parthe and I hosted a tea party. Dull."

All the entries seemed the same. Dull, dull, dull! Finally, she turned to a special entry on a dog-eared page. It read,

"February 7, 1837: God spoke to me and called me to His service."

Florence had read those words so many times since, yet she shivered every time she read them. She recalled how one night, when she was only sixteen years old, she had woken up from her sleep and heard a voice. She knew it was God's voice. Since then she had felt that God wanted her to do something special for Him. The only problem was, she didn't know what.

Florence's Family

Florence, the beautiful city in Italy that inspired Florence Nightingale's name.

Florence and her sister Parthenope were born outside of England. Their parents, Fanny and William Nightingale, were having a three-year honeymoon in Italy. Parthenope was born in Naples in 1819 and named after the original Greek settlement there. Florence was born May 12th, 1820 in the city that inspired her name.

Their father was the son of a successful Sheffield banker, and had been born in Derbyshire in 1795. His original family name was Shore, but he had changed it to Nightingale, after the uncle whose lead mine and country estates he had inherited.

William could enjoy his good fortune without having to work. He liked to read and travel and introduce his family to the most fashionable

Florence's father, William Edward Nightingale.

places in Europe. In England they lived at Lea Hurst, the country home William had inherited.

Florence loved Lea Hurst. But her father decided the house was too small for company — there were only fifteen bedrooms — and besides, it was too remote and cold. So he bought another mansion, Embley Park, in Hampshire. The Nightingale family spent summers at Lea Hurst and winters at Embley Park. They also made several extended visits to London for shopping and entertainment.

The Nightingale sisters grew up surrounded by many cousins, uncles and aunts — and with lots of fun and dinners and parties. Their future was secure. All that was expected of them was to learn to become good wives and mothers and to carry on the proper family traditions.

Lea Hurst, the Nightingales' summer residence.

SEEKING A FUTURE

This had happened many years earlier. Now Florence was almost thirty years old — and still, she didn't know what to do with her life. Oh yes, Mama and Papa knew! They wanted her to learn the latest dances, to look beautiful, and to manage the household successfully so she could someday marry a suitable gentleman and become an entertaining hostess. In fact, for some time now they had long had a certain gentleman in mind for her. And now she had disappointed their high hopes for a nearly perfect match.

Florence had first met Richard Monckton Milnes at a dinner party seven years earlier. Richard was wealthy, intelligent, funny, and had a good-hearted nature. He was always surrounded by numerous devoted friends. He was especially known for the breakfast parties he threw for his many friends at his rooms in Pall Mall — friends who included celebrities and artists.

Richard also had a serious side, though. He was a widely travelled linguist and a politician — and not a bad poet either. As a member of Parliament he was especially interested in reforming the schools. Besides, he was deeply in love with Florence. Her father was hopeful that marriage would cure his daughter's melancholy.

Florence herself was not opposed to

the idea. She adored Richard, and Richard was a frequent guest at the Nightingale residences in London, Lea Hurst and Embley Park. Yet she kept him waiting, and then finally, she turned down his marriage proposal after seven years of courtship. Somehow she felt that marriage would hinder her in following God's call. In those days, a married woman was expected to support her husband's work without pursuing a career of her own. And Florence was not willing to give up the idea that God had called her to do something special — whatever that may be.

"I would never feel fulfilled if I spent my life just supporting him and arranging domestic things," she wrote in her journal. "To be forced to continue my present life without hope of another would be intolerable to me. To give up the chance to form for myself a true and rich life would seem to me like suicide."

HAPPY CHILDHOOD DAYS

One winter evening in 1850, when she had finally dismissed the thought of marriage, Florence sat down in her bedroom and knew the time had come to make a decision. Her life up until then had seemed like a puzzle of scattered pieces. Why couldn't she be happy and careless like her sister Parthe? Why couldn't she be satisfied with the life that satisfied so many people? What was wrong with her? It hurt her to see that she worried and disappointed her parents. Where was the missing piece? Her thoughts flew back to her childhood.

She remembered the happy days when she and her mother went to visit the workers and tenants on their estate at Lea Hurst. How good she had felt when she delivered a ham or fresh vegetables to a family in need! How excited she had been when she was able to comfort a poor child with a bowl of warm soup! How fine it had been when she could nurse a sick animal back to health!

Once, when she was only six years old, she and the vicar had been riding through the countryside when they met a group of farmers talking together. Roger, the shepherd, had looked especially upset.

"What's wrong, Roger?" she asked. "Why are the sheep scattered? Where's your dog Cap?"

"Missy," answered Roger, "the boys threw stones at him and broke his leg, I'm afraid. I'll have to hang him and put him out of his pain."

"Oh no!" said Florence. "Where is he?"

Roger led them to a nearby shed. The collie was lying on the floor. Florence and the vicar examined the leg while Roger went out to find a rope.

"I don't think his leg is broken," said

the vicar relieved. "Florence, I think he can be nursed back to health!"

The two companions cleaned the collie's wounds and put hot compresses on its leg. When the shepherd returned with the rope, Florence announced triumphantly, "Throw away your rope, Roger! Cap will get well!"

Many, many years later, the vicar reminded her of the incident. He wrote, "I wonder whether you remember how, twenty-two years ago, you and I averted the intended hanging of poor old shepherd Smither's dog Cap? I can recollect the pleasure which the saving of the life of a poor dog then gave to your young mind. I was delighted to witness it. It was to me . . . a sign of what you were about to become. . . ."

Rosa, rosae, ro

MASTERING THE BASICS

Florence's heart jumped with joy when she thought about helping suffering people and animals. She remembered how she had even taken great pleasure in picking up Parthe's broken dolls and "caring" for them. She bandaged their "injuries" and "nursed" them by sewing them up and handing them back to her astonished sister.

When she was twelve, her father had begun to divert her childish mind from "useless" to more "useful" things. He decided to take over Parthe and Flo's education. Their mother Fanny had taught them good manners. Now he wanted to teach them about scholarly matters. He wanted his girls to be better educated than most upper-class girls of the day. Since he was a Cambridge graduate himself, he was determined to take them as far as possible. "Not because I want them to pursue a career, of course," he assured their skeptical mother, "but strictly because I intend to make them into as cultured wives and mothers as possible. A husband prefers suitable company, you know."

He arranged a lavishly equipped schoolroom and library where he then taught the two sisters French, German, Italian, Greek and Latin, as well as mathematics, history and philosophy. The library was stocked with classics he wanted his girls to read. Flo excelled and soon mastered the basics, whereas Parthe fell further and further behind. She was more interested in drawing and helping her mother with embroidery and flower arrangements. The two sisters grew farther and farther apart.

"You're pushing them too hard," complained Fanny to her husband. "Studying too much is not good. Not that it has done any harm to Parthe, I believe, but Flo is so unlike her sister."

"No harm comes from learning, my dear Fanny," smiled William.

"Well, it hasn't done Flo any good. She would be happier without it."

"Ah, she'll settle down all right," said William. "Give her some time to find herself."

GOD'S WORK

Later, William would wonder if his wife had been right about Flo. Maybe all the learning had gone to her head and put silly dreams into her mind after all. Lately she had begun to study hospital reports! Florence had acquired hospital and asylum statistics from a Protestant sisterhood in Germany and now she had come up with the idea of starting something similar in England. Meanwhile though, the book her father had recently ordered her to read,

Daughters at Home, with religious advice for discontented daughters, was gathering dust on the shelf.

But no matter how much Florence had wanted to please her parents, she found no rest in following their plan for her life. Now, by the age of thirty, she was more restless than ever — but in the midst of her distress a vision began to unfold. She wanted to relieve the suffering of the poor and sick. She wanted to become a nurse!

"Have you gone mad? This is absolutely out of the question!" thundered her father. "Nursing is not for respectable girls! How can you even think such an ungodly thought, you ungrateful girl?"

"But Father," objected Florence, "I want to become a good and respectable nurse! I have been thinking about going to an infirmary in Salisbury in order to learn the profession."

"I'd rather see you working in the kitchen! But a nurse? Never!"

That was that. Florence leaned back in her chair, arms crossed, and Parthe bent nervously over her drawing while their father continued reading aloud to his daughters from **The London Times**.

Flo did not listen. She was tired of **hearing** about what was going on in the world. Instead, she wanted to be part of it and make a difference. She was becoming more and more convinced that her parents' religion was superficial. She could not accept that serving God meant going to parties and chatting and endless evenings in theaters and concert halls. Dinner parties could not be done to the glory of God when there was so much misery among the poor! To serve God must mean to be a servant and do His work in the world — not to cultivate a spiritual state of mind for its own sake. To be a true Christian must mean more than handing out little food baskets and otherwise, shutting out the suffering of the world. To be a real Christian must mean to give yourself to God first and then follow His calling. Hadn't the Lord Jesus Himself been an example of this?

If God had called her to be different — why had He then seemed to slam every door in her face? The only reason she could think of was that God had found her unworthy of serving Him.

"I shall never do anything," she sighed. "I'm worse than dust and nothing."

That night, as Florence went to bed, she prayed, "Dear God, I'm a sinner and I must have grieved Your Holy Spirit. Is there any hope for me? Please forgive me of my vain and sinful life. I pray that You'll find a way I can be useful to others and to You." Little did she know that, in her lowest moment, God was preparing her for her highest achievements.

Nursing before Flo

There was a good reason why Florence's parents reacted so strongly against her desire to become a nurse. In those days, only poor people stayed in hospitals. The huge wards were overcrowded, filthy, blood-splattered and infested with disease and infection. There was no privacy. The "hospital smell" was not the smell of sanitation but of odors so strong that anyone who entered would get nauseous from the stench. This was before Lister's use of antiseptics and Pasteur's discovery of how germs spread. The surgeons were often wearing coats caked with blood and using dirty knives on their patients, who received no painkilling drugs. The best way to survive the horrors of a hospital was by drinking gin or brandy.

The nurses then were mostly untrained, tough women often with bad reputations — unable to be trusted to carry out the simplest medical duty. They were often alcoholics, with

ce Nightingale

Nursing was not for respectable women, as these 19th century cartoons show.

children they had to care for on their own. Sometimes these women would sleep with the doctors or the patients since they were not given a place of their own to rest, except for wooden cages outside the doors of the wards. Florence once wrote her father that a head nurse had told her that "in the course of her large experience she had never known a nurse who was not drunken and that there was immoral conduct practised in the very wards of which she gave me some awful examples."

The idea of professional nursing originated in the Roman Catholic church where there were special orders of nuns who took upon themselves the task of caring for the sick. These nurses inspired Florence Nightingale by their commitment, thorough training and disciplined way of life.

A VISIT TO ROME

"Good Lord! Flo, what's the matter with you? You look so pale and thin!"

Mrs. Bracebridge stepped back to take a better look at her young friend.

"Florence has been suffering from migraines and bronchitis lately," her mother apologized.

"I think she needs a change of climate," Mrs. Bracebridge said. "Flo, why don't you come with me and my husband to Rome? That will do you good."

Florence's parents liked the idea. A visit to the Eternal City might help her forget her silly ideas. They gave their permission for the trip.

The plan seemed to work. During the months in Rome, Florence was temporarily distracted from her obsession with hospital work. Together with the Bracebridges she visited ancient monuments, churches, museums and art galleries. She loved every minute of it, and was especially fascinated by the ceiling paintings in the Sistine Chapel. She spent a whole day staring at them while Mrs. Bracebridge wrote letters in the pew. It was like looking straight into heaven and seeing the angels, prophets and God Himself.

"Of all my days in Rome," she wrote afterwards, "this one has been the happiest and most glorious."

While in Rome, something even more important happened to Florence. She was introduced to a fellow Englishman, Sidney Herbert, the former British secretary of war. Herbert was the person God had chosen to open the door of opportunity for Florence. From the beginning, Herbert wholeheartedly supported her vision of hospital reform and gave her the names and addresses of people who thought along the same lines back in England.

"They're all very respected people. They'll help you," he smiled. Then he added, "Your parents can hardly object to them!"

LEAVING THE NEST

When Florence returned to her family in England again she felt stronger than ever. Her new friends had helped her gather reports on institutions and hospitals from all over Europe. She soon knew more about health care than anyone else. Because she knew her parents disliked her interest in medical matters, she would get up before dawn to study hundreds of pages of reports on statistics about the outbreak of diseases, nutrition or drainage problems. Then when her family woke up, she joined them for breakfast and assumed her domestic and social duties. Then, whenever she had a

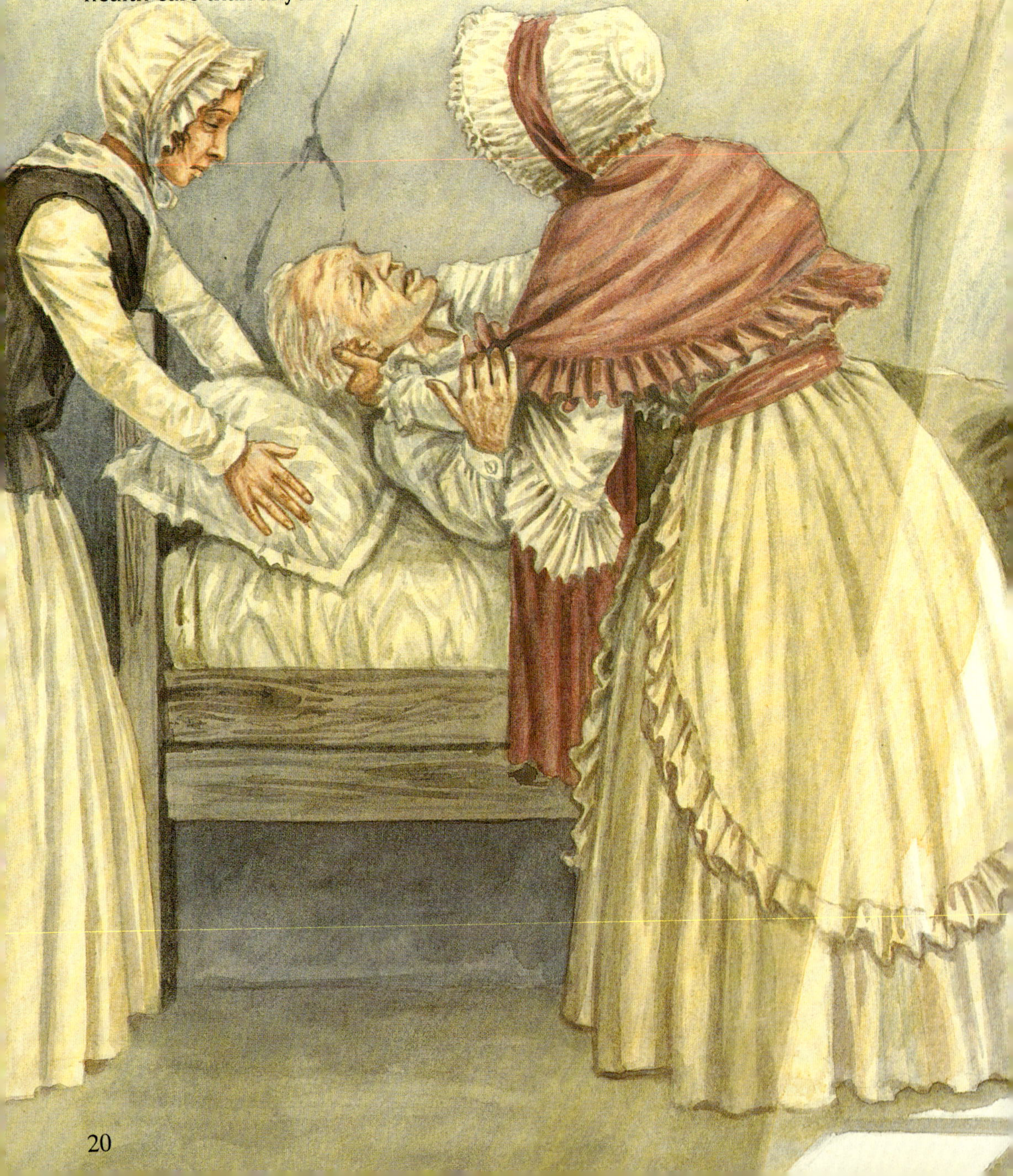

chance she would go off to care for sick relatives or visit the poor in nearby villages.

"Alas, we're ducks," wailed her mother, "but we've hatched a wild swan!"

She was wrong. It was not a swan Fanny and William had hatched. It was an eagle. And the eagle was about to soar.

A Visit to Kaiserwerth

When Florence was 31 years old she had the chance to visit the Institution of Deaconesses at Kaiserswerth near Dusseldorf, Germany — while her mother and Parthe had mud cures at a famous resort in Carlsbad (presently called Karlovy Vary). The Kaiserswerth institution was inspired by the work of Roman Catholic nuns, but run by Protestants. It had a hospital, two schools, an orphanage and an asylum for the mentally ill. The women serving there were mostly single or widowed women who wanted to serve out of their Christian faith.

At Kaiserswerth Florence received her first professional training. She had to get up at 5 a.m. and work till noon before she had a ten-minute lunch break when she ate broth and vegetables. She had another short break with tea and bread at 3 p.m., and finally the workday would end with one more bowl of broth at 7 p.m. The evenings were spent studying the Bible. Florence took all the training there was to be had at Kaiserswerth since there was nothing similar in England.

"I am as happy as the day is long," she wrote home. "Now I know what it is to live and to love life!"

But the joy was short-lived. After three months she had to go back to London to join her family. Her mother hardly spoke to her — and Parthe did not know what to think of her sister.

NURSE AT LAST!

In the summer of 1853, when Florence was thirty-three years old, she finally had a chance to break loose from her family and test her wings. The Institution for the Care of Sick Gentlewomen in Distressed Circumstances in London was setting up a hospital on Harley Street. A superintendent was needed and Sidney Herbert's wife suggested Florence Nightingale. Her family fought the proposal in every way they could.

"Florence, what will people say?" wailed her mother while almost fainting.

"But Mother," protested Florence, "this is a sanatorium for sick governesses. And it's managed by a committee of fine ladies."

"But Flo, you have absolutely no practical experience in running a sanatorium!" interrupted Parthe.

"Please Parthe," sighed her father, "you shouldn't interfere in your sister's affairs."

The atmosphere was poisoned with hysteria and threats. Yet Florence did not budge. She packed her bags and carried them down to the carriage waiting outside. Her father came outside to say good-bye.

"May God be with you, Flo," he said and added, "I'll make sure you receive an allowance of £500 ($1000) a year!"

Florence was on her way.

APPRENTICESHIP IN HARLEY STREET

Florence Nightingale surveyed the empty house at number 1 Harley Street. No beds, no furniture, no kitchenware, no curtains, no linen, no nurses! In ten days the patients would move in.

"By the way," said the chairman of the ladies' committee sponsoring the hospital, "we see fit that only members of the Church of England be admitted."

"We shall see," answered Florence quietly but firmly. "I think this place will be proper for any woman who is sick and poor — regardless of her faith!"

The ladies thought this new superintendent had some very strange ideas. "Only good women make good nurses," she insisted. In her opinion, the comfort of the patients and the well-being of the nurses were important for success, as were healthy nutrition, order and cleanliness. During her fourteen months as

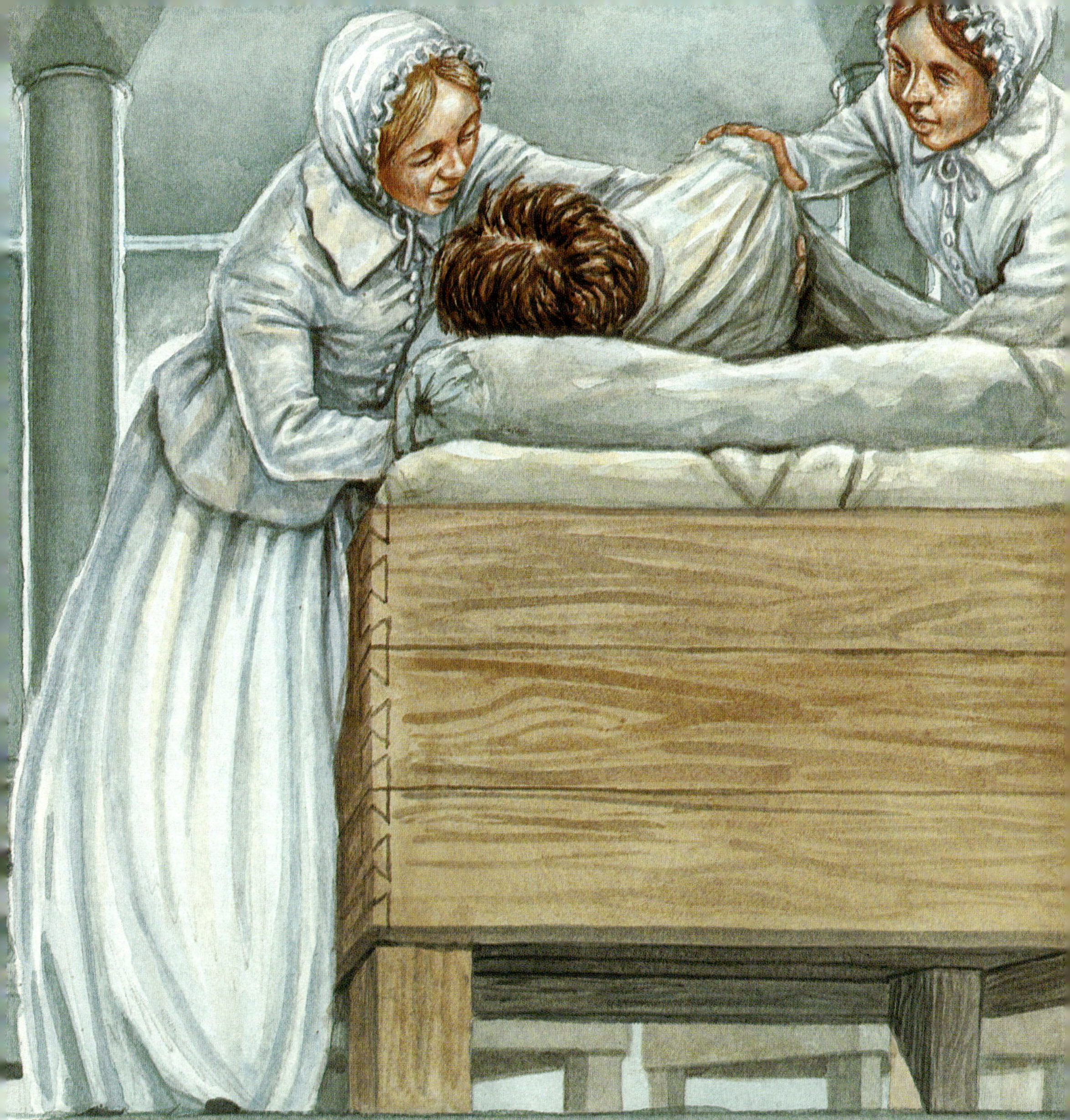

superintendent, Miss Nightingale modernized the profession of nursing. She invented bells for the patients to call their nurse — "a valve which flies open when the bell rings, and remains open in order that the nurse may see who has rung." She installed a food elevator to haul the patients' meals up to the wards from the kitchen. She bought food and supplies at bulk rate, organized jam making in the kitchen to save money, set up a laundry room and carefully selected her staff.

"I am now in the heyday of my power," she wrote to her father.

The ladies' committee was astounded. Instead of the ministering angel they had expected they were dealing with a human dynamo who was revolutionizing the concept of hospital work. Their superintendent had even managed to manipulate the men's committee out from behind the scenes in order to have her way. Miss Nightingale always won.

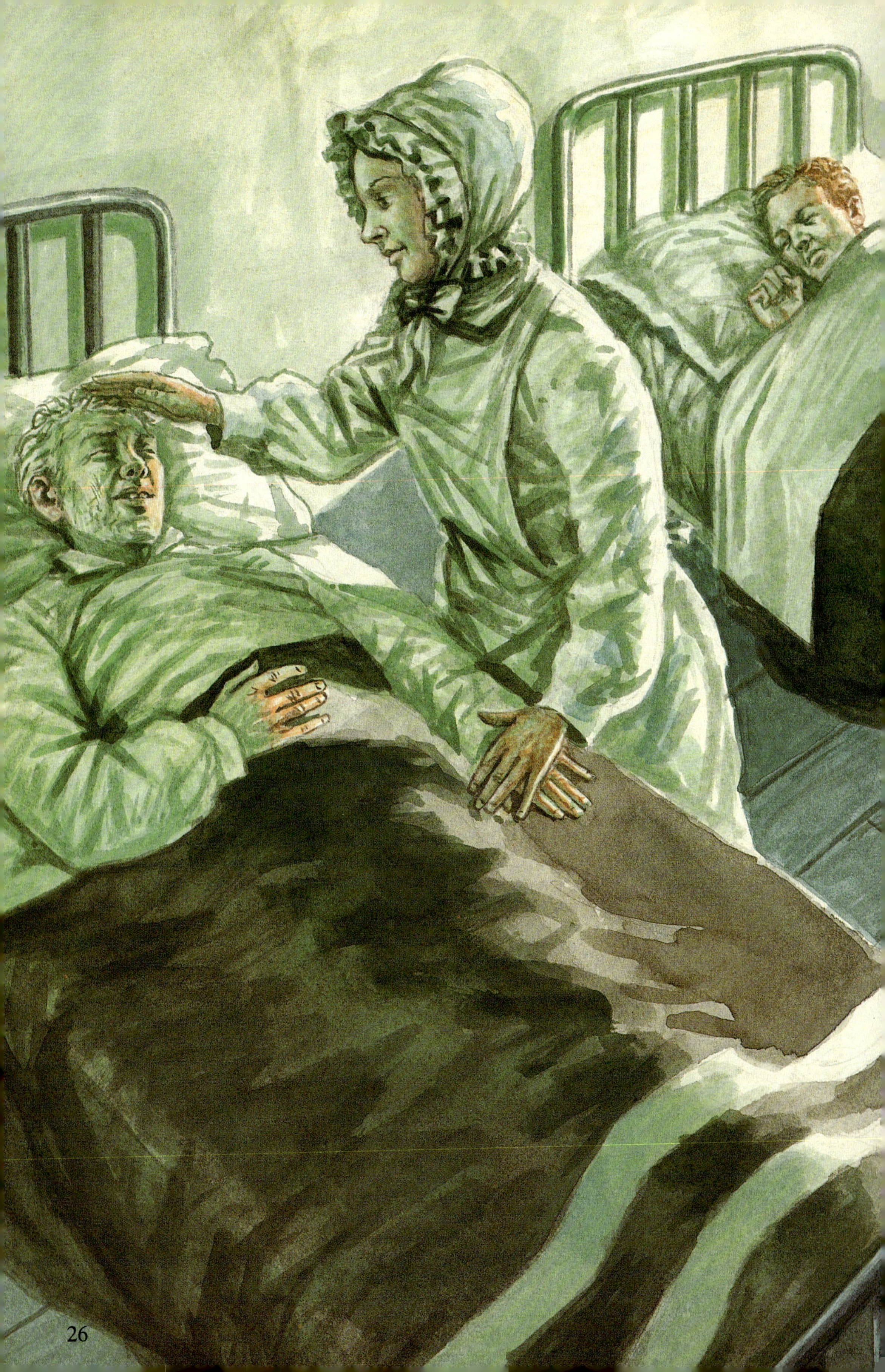

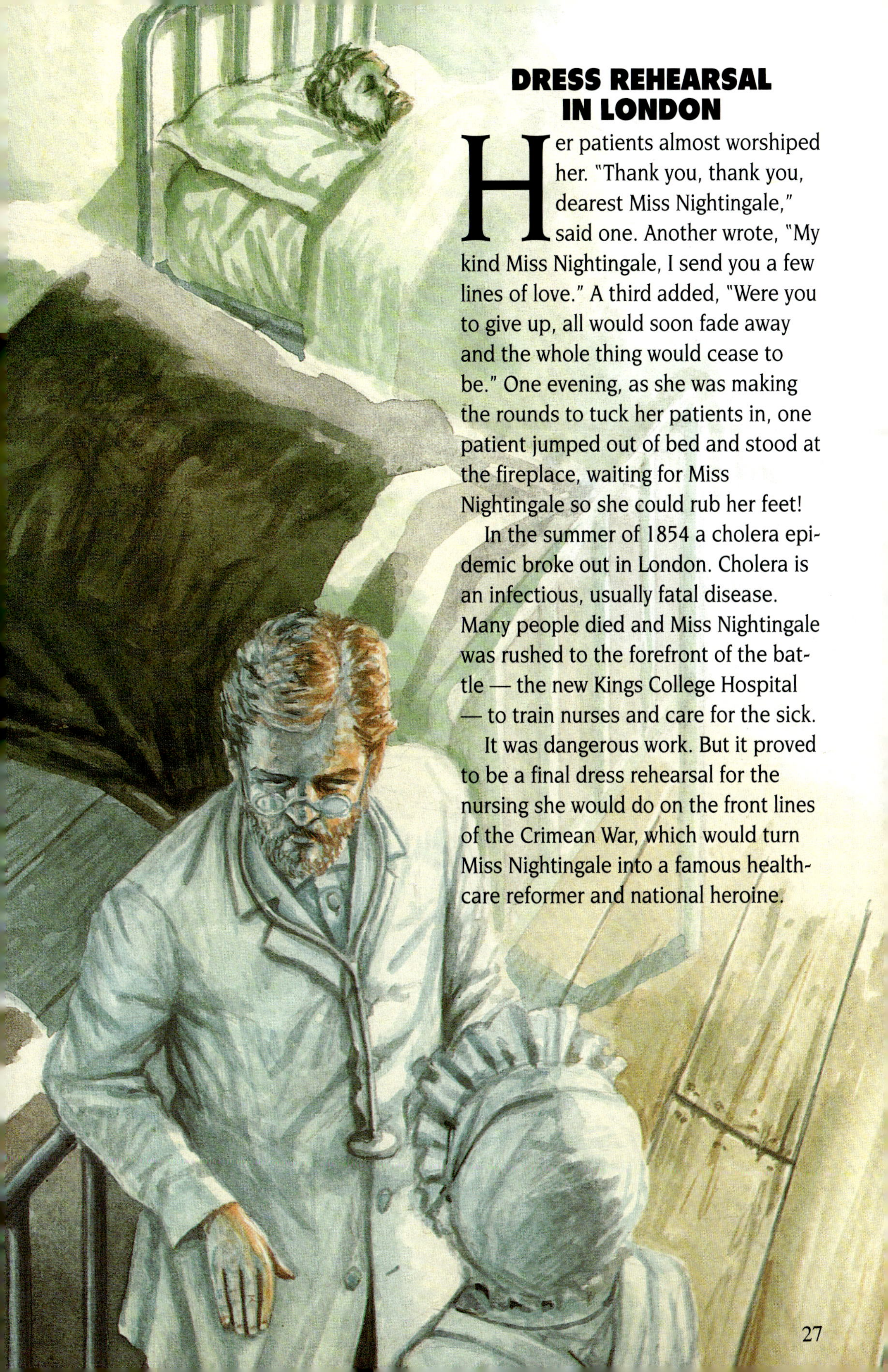

DRESS REHEARSAL IN LONDON

Her patients almost worshiped her. "Thank you, thank you, dearest Miss Nightingale," said one. Another wrote, "My kind Miss Nightingale, I send you a few lines of love." A third added, "Were you to give up, all would soon fade away and the whole thing would cease to be." One evening, as she was making the rounds to tuck her patients in, one patient jumped out of bed and stood at the fireplace, waiting for Miss Nightingale so she could rub her feet!

In the summer of 1854 a cholera epidemic broke out in London. Cholera is an infectious, usually fatal disease. Many people died and Miss Nightingale was rushed to the forefront of the battle — the new Kings College Hospital — to train nurses and care for the sick.

It was dangerous work. But it proved to be a final dress rehearsal for the nursing she would do on the front lines of the Crimean War, which would turn Miss Nightingale into a famous healthcare reformer and national heroine.

APPEAL FROM THE BATTLEFIELD

It all began the following fall when war broke out between England and Russia. British soldiers were shipped to the island of Crimea in the Black Sea in an attempt to besiege Sevastopol and defeat their enemy. A British war correspondent, William Howard Russell, sent alarming eyewitness accounts, together with an appeal for help, back to The London Times — the first war coverage by a journalist ever.

"The wounded have just been left on the field," wrote Russell, "some for two nights, all of them for at least one. From the battlefield they have been bundled on board a ship for transport across the Black Sea to Scutari without medical attention. . . . The neglected gunshot wounds bred maggots, which crawled in every direction, infecting the food of the unhappy beings on board. The putrid animal matter caused such a stench that the officers and crew were nearly overcome, and the captain is now ill from the effects of the five days of misery. . . . The men must attend to each other or receive

no relief at all. . . . Are there no devoted women among us, able and willing to go forth and minister to the sick and suffering soldiers of the East?"

England was apalled. Their young men were dying like flies abroad — some from battle wounds, but more than sixty per cent were dying from curable diseases and a simple lack of medical attention. There was a desperate need for immediate relief work. Sidney Herbert, now British secretary at war, sent a hasty letter to his friend Miss Nightingale.

"There is only one person in England I know of who is capable of organizing the hospital work in Scutari," he wrote. "This person is you. Would you please go and oversee the entire situation?"

Within 48 hours after Russell's appeal in the Times, Miss Nightingale was ready to go. With her went a housekeeper, the Bracebridges and the best thirty-eight women she could find — some were regular hospital nurses, others were Catholic nuns and there were also Anglican nuns — all going to care for the wounded soldiers at Scutari.

Miss Nightingale's War Nurses

"Forty British females are more difficult to manage than 4,000 men!" said Florence Nightingale about her Scutari nurses.

They certainly were a hastily chosen and somewhat ill-fitting team — some were coarse, untrained women, others Roman Catholic nuns and Protestant sisters. The religious nurses would often argue over doctrine and sometimes accuse each other of preaching their own beliefs among the soldiers. The non-religious nurses often lacked self-discipline and proper conduct. In fact, ten of them were sent home shortly after they arrived because of inappropriate moral behavior.

The uniform was a gray tweed jacket, cap and skirt, woolen cloak, brown scarf embroidered in red with the words "Scutari Hospital" — an unattractive outfit that would help "protect" the nurses from male admirers among the patients and hospital staff.

A month after their arrival, Florence Nightingale was notified that another team of 47 nurses was on its way. The Lady-in-Chief was furious. This was more than she could handle. Besides, there were no accommodations for them.

"I have toiled my way," she wrote her boss Sidney Herbert, "into the confidence of the medical men. I have introduced something like a system into the disorderly operations of these women. But to have women scampering about the wards of a military hospital all day long, which they would do if an increased number relax the discipline and increase their leisure, would be as improper as absurd."

The Lady-in-Chief received the new nurses coldly and shuffeled the old and new packs, sending thirty of them to Crimea and keeping fifty in Scutari.

Eventually she sent for more nurses, and before the war was over the nursing staff at Scutari had grown to 125.

One of Russell's dispatches for The London Times.

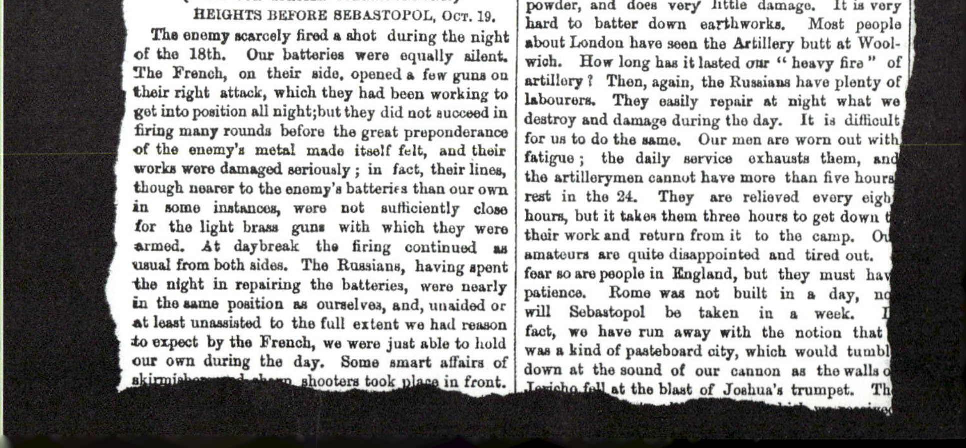

THE

WAR IN THE CRIMEA.

THE OPERATIONS OF THE SIEGE.

[The following appeared in our second edition of yesterday:—]

(FROM OUR SPECIAL CORRESPONDENT.)

HEIGHTS BEFORE SEBASTOPOL, OCT. 19.

The enemy scarcely fired a shot during the night of the 18th. Our batteries were equally silent. The French, on their side, opened a few guns on their right attack, which they had been working to get into position all night; but they did not succeed in firing many rounds before the great preponderance of the enemy's metal made itself felt, and their works were damaged seriously; in fact, their lines, though nearer to the enemy's batteries than our own in some instances, were not sufficiently close for the light brass guns with which they were armed. At daybreak the firing continued as usual from both sides. The Russians, having spent the night in repairing the batteries, were nearly in the same position as ourselves, and, unaided or at least unassisted to the full extent we had reason to expect by the French, we were just able to hold our own during the day. Some smart affairs of skirmishers and sharp shooters took place in front. of this officer, whose name may be familiar to some readers in connexion with the Sinope expedition.

OCTOBER 20.

Two 68 pounders were mounted last night in our batteries, and the firing, which nearly ceased after dark, was renewed by daybreak. We are all getting tired of this continual "pound-pounding," which makes a great deal of noise, wastes much powder, and does very little damage. It is very hard to batter down earthworks. Most people about London have seen the Artillery butt at Woolwich. How long has it lasted our "heavy fire" of artillery? Then, again, the Russians have plenty of labourers. They easily repair at night what we destroy and damage during the day. It is difficult for us to do the same. Our men are worn out with fatigue; the daily service exhausts them, and the artillerymen cannot have more than five hours rest in the 24. They are relieved every eight hours, but it takes them three hours to get down to their work and return from it to the camp. Our amateurs are quite disappointed and tired out. I fear so are people in England, but they must have patience. Rome was not built in a day, nor will Sebastopol be taken in a week. In fact, we have run away with the notion that it was a kind of pasteboard city, which would tumble down at the sound of our cannon as the walls of Jericho fell at the blast of Joshua's trumpet. Th

The Crimean War

In 1853 Russia attacked the Turkish Empire in order to gain access to the Mediterranean from the Black Sea. In March the following year England and France sided with Turkey and declared war on Russia. Six months later the allies landed 50,000 troops on the Crimean peninsula and surrounded the strong Russian naval base at Sevastopol. The Russians lost several bloody battles, but not without inflicting heavy casualties on the allies who had already abandoned much of their equipment, including medical supplies. To make matters worse, deadly diseases such as typhus and cholera broke out, leaving the allies in chaos — despite their success on the battlefield. Unlike the French who had brought trained nuns and nurses with them, the British army proved totally incapable of coping with their sick and wounded. All they had was an ambulance corps of old pensioners. Florence Nightingale and her nurses were desperately needed!

The war dragged on until February 1856 when Austria finally joined the allied forces. Russia then capitulated and signed a treaty forcing it to abandon its naval bases on the Black Sea.

Top: War correspondent William Howard Russell. Middle: British and Russian soldiers fight the battle of Balaklava, October 25th, 1854. Bottom: The Crimean winter captured by the new medium of photography. Russell reporting in his tent while Florence Nightingale awaits wounded soldiers.

CHAOS AT SCUTARI

Miss Nightingale was optimistic — despite her ill-equipped and diverse band of nurses. Sidney Herbert had assured her that plenty of supplies had been sent on ahead — tons of lint, 15,000 pairs of sheets, medicine, wine, arrowroot, food and everything else needed to run an effective army hospital. There were also plenty of doctors — one to every ninety-five men — the highest proportion on a British battlefield ever.

Two weeks later, Miss Nightingale's rescue team landed on the shores just down the coast from the Turkish village of Scutari. Rain was pouring down and black clouds hung over an enormous, ugly building on top of the hill. This was the army barracks where the wounded had been brought. It looked more like a prison than a hospital.

Once again, Miss Nightingale came up against an impossible situation: The supplies promised her were nowhere to be found! Evidently, they had bypassed Scutari and either been confiscated by Turkish customs agents, or just disappeared somewhere in Crimea! There were no sheets! Hardly any blankets! No heat! No soap, no clean water, no towels, and no clothing! No furniture or tables — not even an operation table! No food except for chunks of meat full of gristle and fat! No kitchenware! Only one kitchen with thirteen copperpots to serve 2,500 patients! The place was overcrowded and filthy, infested with lice, maggots and disease. There were rats everywhere. The walls steamed with damp. From the sewers underneath the building rose a stinking odor which the cold wind blew up through the pipes into the wards.

And in addition to all this, the medical staff already there hardly welcomed the nurses with open arms. The medical officer in charge and the military commandant gave the nurses nothing more than a professional handshake. There was an obvious prejudice against women interfering in men's affairs. And here were two reasons for the men to be upset. Both war, and wounded soldiers belonged strictly to the men's world. Female amateur nurses were not wanted — especially when it meant that neglect and inefficiency would be exposed! The doctors forbade the nurses to enter the wards where the wounded lay, unless they were specifically asked to. So Miss Nightingale obeyed and ordered her helpers to clean and organize as much of the building as they could. Little by little she won over the doctors purely through her quiet and determined way of doing things.

One evening, as she was discussing a certain matter with a doctor, the doctor snarled, "But that's impossible! This cannot be done!"

"But Doctor," came the quiet reply, "it must be done!"

Then unforeseen events lowered the doctors' resistance even further. When a new battle was fought at Balaclava, a flood of wounded men were brought to the hospital at Scutari. Now the doctors had no choice. They needed all the help they could get.

THE LADY WITH THE LAMP

Miss Nightingale's nurses were finally permitted to do the work they had come for. They worked round the clock

among the sick and wounded — the Lady-in-Chief often twenty hours a day! Wherever suffering was at its worst and the need for help was greatest — there was Miss Nightingale! Night after night she walked with her lantern down the four miles of corridors and wards to check on the sick. She often sat down by a bedside to write a letter for a soldier unable to write himself — or to hold the hand of a dying man.

"I've seen her spend hours with men dying of cholera, or fever," said one patient. "Her slight form could be seen bending over them, administering to their ease in every way in her power, and seldom quitting their sides until death had released them."

Her mere presence and personal attention brought healing and hope. Not even the roughest soldier dared to swear in her presence.

"What a comfort it was even to see her pass by," remembered one man. "She would speak to one and nod and smile to many more. But she could not do it to all, you know, we lay there by the hundreds; but we could kiss her shadow as it fell, and lay our heads on the pillow again, content."

ORDER OUT OF CHAOS

And so, after six months of hard labor, the Lady-in-Chief could step back and evaluate all that had been accomplished: The mortality rate among soldiers had fallen drastically — from fourty-two per cent to two; the patients were properly clothed; the mattresses were covered with clean linen; the kitchens were organized; the hunks of meat had been replaced with well-prepared and appetizing meals; a laundry was running efficiently; a storehouse had been established with plenty of supplies; the sanitary system had been improved; and a new ward had been built.

But the Lady-in-Chief was still not satisfied. "I have been clothing the British army," she wrote Sidney Herbert. Now the time had come to care for her patients' spiritual needs.

A readingroom was furnished, and recreational activities started. There were even classes to educate the sol-

diers and their families. The officers were amazed to see how the Lady-in-Chief treated their men.

"She's spoiling the brutes!" grinned one officer.

She was not spoiling them. She was treating them with love and dignity and helping them become better human beings.

It almost cost her her life, though. During a visit to the battlefields at Balaclava, Miss Nightingale fell ill with "Crimean fever." She was carried on a stretcher to a nearby hospital, where the doctors did not think she would live much longer. When the news reached the hospital at Scutari, the men turned their faces to the walls and cried.

But the stubborn Lady-in-Chief was determined to recover. And recover she did — only to work more eagerly than ever before. In the summer of 1856, when the war finally ended, she left her last "children" in Scutari, and sailed back to England.

A NATIONAL HEROINE

A heroine's welcome awaited her. England wanted to celebrate their brave nurse. Military bands, triumphal arches, speeches and banquets were planned. Instead though, she managed to slip undetected into her homeland — disguised as a "Miss Smith."

She caught a train for Derbyshire and walked to Lea Hurst, her childhood home, where she took her family by surprise.

"Flo! My daughter!" beamed her mother. "The whole of England is welcoming you!"

"Welcome home," added her father. "We're proud of you, Florence!"

The next morning the bells at the village church announced her homecoming. England was ringing with her name. But Florence was not impressed by all the fuss. Her heart was still with the many soldiers who had died of neglect back in the hospital barracks at Scutari and Crimea.

That night she wrote in her journal, "I am standing before the altar of murdered men. As long as I live I will fight their cause."

VISITING THE QUEEN

And fight she did — determined that only thorough reform of the army medical service would prevent a repetition of the Crimean War fiasco. The following year she drew up an alarming report for the Royal Commission on the Health of the British Army — a committee she herself had helped appoint, with Sidney Herbert as chairman. The 1,000-page report was full of statistics and observations from army hospitals she had visited. The document was accompanied with this personal note from her days at Scutari: "No one can feel for the Army as I do. These people who talk to us have all fed their children on the fat of the land and dressed them in velvet and silk while we have been away. I have had to see my 'children' dressed in dirty blankets and old pairs of regimental trousers, and to see them fed on raw, salted meat. Nine thousand of my 'children' are lying from causes which might have been prevented in their forgotten graves. But I can never forget. . . ."

In those days it was still unthinkable for a woman to enter politics. So Florence Nightingale had to do her reform work from behind the scenes by bullying reluctant politicians to take up her cause. In the fall of 1856 she was invited to see Queen Victoria and Prince Albert and went fully armed with facts and plans, to plead her case at the highest level. The queen gave her a brooch with the inscription, "Blessed are the merciful."

After the audience the prince said, "She put before us all the defects of our present military hospital system, and the reforms that are needed. We are much pleased with her. She is extremely modest."

Queen Victoria remarked, "I wish we had her at the War Office!"

HEALTH REFORMS

Over the next few years many reforms followed — due to Florence Nightingale's persistence. In 1859 the War Office established a medical college in Kent. In 1861 a military hospital was opened in London. And the following year a permanent army sanitary commission was set up to make sure that the new practices were kept up to standard. In 1857, when the Indian army rebelled against British rule, another commission was appointed to ensure the soldiers' welfare in India.

Florence Nightingale was involved in all of this. But most of all, she was interested in reforming the nursing education itself, so in 1860 the Nightingale School for Nurses was opened in London.

Reforms in India

Florence Nightingale never set foot on Indian soil — and yet she came to be known as the "Governess of India" because of the important reform work she did for this former British colony.

The British first came to India as peaceful traders. But when the Mughal empire collapsed, the British took control, claiming the need to prevent crime and civil war. By the middle of the nineteenth century, law and order had been reestablished and a new Indian army under British command was in place.

Even though life for the Indians was hard under British rule, the British started many important projects to improve living conditions in India: construction of roads and railroads, canals to drain swamps and irrigate dry land, schools and hospitals. Yet many Indians preferred their traditional way of life. This led to a brief national uprising in 1857 which was put down by the British.

Florence Nightingale was deeply concerned for the welfare of the army and the general population in India. Two years after she returned from Scutari she began to work towards establishing a Sanitary Commission for India, headed by her friend Sidney Herbert. A questionnaire she drafted was sent out to every military station in the colony. When the

results came in, she analyzed them herself, then wrote a 2,000-page report, entitled **Observations by Miss Nightingale**. This comprehensive report discussed over-crowding in barracks, hygiene, water, diet, exercise, disease, drainage, hospitals and, of course, mortality statistics.

"The picture is terrible," admitted the commission, "but it's all true!"

Over the next twenty-five years, Florence Nightingale's reform ideas for the army developed into a program of reform for the entire public health administration of India — inspired by her next book, **How People May Live and not Die in India**. Every step of health progress taken in India during the latter part of the nineteenth century — military as well as civil — was more due to Florence Nightingale than any other man or woman.

The Nightingale School for Nurses

When Florence Nightingale returned from Scutari many people wanted to support her work for the sick and poor. A fund was set up and money poured in from people who supported her idea of starting a training school for nurses.

During this planning stage Florence Nightingale wrote **Notes on Nursing: What It is and What It is Not**. The book offered a great deal of practical advice and became extremely popular. More than any of her other books, this one helped outline a professional training program.

The Nightingale nursing school opened at St. Thomas' Hospital on June 24th 1860, when fifteen applicants were chosen for the one-year course. Thirteen of them qualified to become certified nurses. The trainees were instructed by physicians and surgeons in not only bed-making, dressing of wounds and other simple skills, but also in the very scientific basis of their work.

The school became a great success. "I trust that our school may lead the way towards supplying a want long felt in England," said Florence Nightingale. New schools sprang up all over the country — even in other countries. The modern nursing profession is a result of Florence Nightingale's ideas.

This photo of a ward in St. Thomas' Hospital in London shows Florence Nightingale's lasting influence on the profession of nursing.

THE FINAL YEARS

Florence Nightingale never fully recovered from her exhausting years in Scutari. Even though she lived another fifty years, she was often sick and bedridden. As her sight failed, she withdrew from public life, cared for her parents till they died, and wrote many letters. These she often concluded with, "If I can be of any use, here I am."

Three years before her death, King Edward VII presented her with the Order of Merit, the highest honor a British civilian could obtain. Florence Nightingale was the first woman ever to receive the award, but it hardly meant anything to her.

"Too kind, too kind," she murmured.

At 90, she died peacefully in her sleep — lonely and almost forgotten by the general public. She had not wanted

a hero's burial in Westminster Abbey, only that her body would be used for dissection in a training hospital, but this wish was ignored. Instead she was buried next to her mother and father near Embley Park. The words on the memorial stone read, "F.N. Born 1820. Died 1910."

A couragous woman with extraordinary gifts and powers had passed through the world and left it a better place for us all. Thanks to her brave determination and stubborn love, thousands had been nurtured back to health — and nursing had been revolutionized and changed forever into an honorable profession.

Main Events in Florence's Life

1820	12 May	Born in Florence, Italy.
1837		Tours the European continent. Called to serve God. Victoria becomes queen.
1839		Presented at the queen's court.
1842	10 May	Introduced to Richard Monckton Milnes at a party.
1844		First hospital visits.
1845		Parents object to training at Salisbury Infirmary.
1847	Dec.	Visits Catholic hospitals in Rome, Italy.
1849		Decides not to marry Richard but pursue God's calling instead.
1850	August	Brief visit to Kaiserwerth.
1851	July	Training at Kaiserwerth.
1853	August	Superintendent of the Institution for the Care of Sick Gentlewomen in London.
1854	March	The Crimean War breaks out.
	October	Appointed to lead nursing mission to Scutari.
	November	Arrives in Scutari. Visits Balaklava.
1855	June	Seriously ill with Crimean fever. The Nightingale Fund set up in England to assist her work.
1856	March	The Crimean War ends.
	August	Returns to England. Meets Queen Victoria and Prince Albert.
1857		Rebellion in India. Royal Commission set up to investigate the army medical service.
1859		Notes on Hospitals (about hospital design) and Notes on Nursing (about guidelines and conduct) published.
1860	9 July	The Nightingale Training School opens in London.
1861	October	Helps the United States organize hospitals during the Civil War. Sidney Herbert dies.
1865		Moves into her Mayfair home in London, given to her by her father.
1868		Helps establish East London Nursing Society.
1871		Appointed head of the Nightingale Training School.
1874		Death of her father.
1880		Death of her mother.
1890		Death of Parthe.
1901		Loses eyesight. Queen Victoria dies.
1907	Dec.	Awarded Order of Merit.
1910	13 August	Florence Nightingale dies peacefully in her sleep.

THE CRIMEAN BATTLEFIELDS

BOOK RESOURCES

Florence Nightingale: God's Servant at the Battlefield, by David R. Collins (Mott Media, 1985).
Florence Nightingale: The Lady of the Lamp, by Basil Miller (Bethany).
Florence Nightingale, by Dorothy Turner (The Bookwright Press, 1986).
Florence Nightingale, by Richard Tames (Franklin Watts, 1989).
Florence Nightingale, by Irene Cooper Willis (Coward-McCann, 1931).
Florence Nightingale, by Elspeth Huxley (G.P.Putnam's Sons, 1975)
Eminent Victorians, by Lytton Strachey (Weidenfeld & Nicolson, 1989).